Spring Cleaning *Me*

A Key to Effectiveness in Your Purpose

Foreword by Sam and Vicki Farina

Spring Cleaning *Me*

A Key to Effectiveness in Your Purpose

By Aileen Price

To my Lord and Savior, who loves me like no one else could, who guides me in His righteous ways, and who redeems my darkest days. You are my source and my EVERYTHING. May my life be a sacrifice pleasing to You.

Coach Approach Ministries, you have blessed me by training me in my career passion. Thank you for giving life to my vision and my aspirations. Thank you for allowing me to share this message. Bill Copper, thank you for guiding me through the publication process.

Acknowledgements

To Ann Arbor Assembly of God: Pastor Bill, thank you for your patient mentorship and unconditional godly love. You empowered me; you recognized my calling and gave me a chance. Kim, thank you for sharing your powerful testimony of divine healing through the power of the Word and the renewal of your mind. Your story captures the essence of *Spring Cleaning Me.* A3oG friends, thank for believing in me and helping me grow in my calling.

To my family: Christopher, my love, thank you for not letting me settle for anything less than God's best for me. Mami, you've taught me through example to pursue God earnestly with reckless abandon. Daddy, though you're with the Lord, your love and belief in me compel me to boldly aim for the stars. Angelo, thank you for urging me to put the "boxing gloves back on and to get back into the ring."

To my coaching trainers and mentors: Mary Selzer, Vicki and Sam Farina, Bill Copper, and Nancy Branton. You've given me tools to be a professional coach and a minister of personal growth.

Marlene Moore, Toni Moore (unrelated), and Ken Liples, thank you for your proofreading and edits.

To CityLife Church: Pastor Brad, thank you for praying with me during writer's block. CityLife friends, you energize me!

Spring Cleaning *Me*

Contents

Foreword

FROM THE MIND OF SAM

The origin of spring cleaning can be traced to the ancient Jewish practice of thoroughly cleansing the home in anticipation of the spring time memorial feast of Passover. Observant Jews conduct a thorough "spring cleaning" of the house searching for *chametz*, the smallest crumb that may contain leaven. They are expressly commanded to rid their home of even the tiniest particle that represents sin in the house. Chametz is considered a corrupting influence, a hidden uncleanness that manipulates purer elements. Like the influence of a lump of leaven in dough, "spiritual" leaven functions as an evil impulse within us that corrupts and/or "sours" our soul. The entire family gets involved in this sacred act. They search for bread crumbs under cushions of sofas and chairs, clean the oven and stove, and even refrigerator and freezer.

FROM THE HEART OF VICKI

When I first saw Aileen sitting in the back of a room of leaders, gathered to develop their skills in Christian coaching, I was drawn to her. I instantly knew she had a story that needed to be told. What was different about her story? Aileen is a young woman with a past (just like all of us)--even with some secret leavened crumbs. Aileen came to know and fell in love with a man named Jesus who continually told her past didn't matter. He was only concerned about her future. He became the love of her heart, and today she tells her "spring cleaning" story in such a beautiful iconic way.

Aileen portrays a modern day type of David— "A woman after God's own heart." She echoes the words from Psalms 51:7-12[ESV]: "Purge me with hyssop, and I shall be clean; wash me, and I shall be whiter than snow. Let me hear joy and gladness; let the bones that you have broken rejoice. Hide your face from my sins, and blot out all my iniquities. Create in me a clean heart, O God, and renew a right spirit within me. Cast me not away from your presence, and take not your Holy Spirit from me. Restore to me the joy of your salvation, and uphold me with a willing spirit."

How do we remove the "chametz" from our mind, heart, and soul? Drawing from her own life experiences and her love for Christ and others, these are the spiritual truths Aileen wishes to answer in her book, *Spring Cleaning Me*. She is not afraid to delve into the dark corners, or lift the cushions of the chairs and sofas of our lives that are often overlooked. This is a wonderful blueprint for cleaning the human mind and soul. *Spring Cleaning Me* is "must read" for every one, and we pray for its widest circulation.

Sam and Vicki Farina
Sam Farina Ministries

Spring Cleaning *Me*

Preface

As I reflect on the journey culminating in this book, I'm in awe of the Lord's hand carefully placing each piece of the puzzle in its place. The concept for *Spring Cleaning Me* was birthed in early 2011. Pastor Bill at Ann Arbor Assembly of God (A3oG) granted me the opportunity to organize two women's conferences around topics burning in my heart. In October 2010, we gathered to discuss one's purpose and place not only within the body of Christ but also and within one's community. During that event, Pastor Bill asked me to organize another conference for the spring.

Over the next several weeks, my heart was filled with the title "Spring Cleaning *Me*". The theme verses became Psalm 139:23-24: "Search me, God, and know my heart; test me and know my anxious thoughts. See if there is any offensive way in me, and lead me in the way everlasting." The vision for this conference was fueled by an urgency in my spirit: in order for us to be promoted spiritually, we had to be stripped of any "offensive ways" within us. At the time, I didn't see the connection between the two events. In hindsight, I see how the Lord used the first conference to make us think intently about our purpose. The second was a call to position ourselves strategically on the path to fulfilling that purpose with effectiveness.

During my personal devotions and preparation for the Bible classes I taught, I read books in which I saw a distinct pattern in the lives of high profile ministers. In each book, I noticed the authors underwent a time of preparation prior to the launch of their ministries or prior to embarking on a new phase within their ministries. These times of preparation included a time of cleaning, renewing their spirits, and drawing closer to Him.

As I read the pages of those books, I felt the Holy Spirit nudging me saying, "You need to do this too." I became inspired to devote time specifically for the purpose of allowing God to change me from the inside out, knowing the process would be completely worth any discomfort or growing pains I'd experience. Around that time, I had embraced my calling. I'd yielded my will to His. By submitting to Him, I received clarity for my life. I was ready to go to any lengths necessary to pursue my calling. I poured my whole being into my purpose, much like I'd done for my education and building my career.

The outcome of my study is reflected in the pages of this book. I've discovered that the journey of our purpose and our spiritual development is a life-long process. I've learned that just as the year has seasons so does our spiritual development. There are seasons that appear dormant, as if nothing were happening. There are seasons when we see buds coming through the tough ground of faithful expectancy. The third chapter of Ecclesiastes emphasizes there's a time for everything, and I've come to embrace that all times are equally important. Ecclesiastes 3:3 says there's "a time to tear down and a time to build".

Your soul's health and integrity depend on maintaining it nourished and carefully groomed. Consider *Spring Cleaning Me* a time to tear down the ungodly and to build up according to the Spirit. It's a time to clear the soul free of clutter. It's a time to embrace the freedom that will empower you to fulfill your life's purpose successfully. May you blessed and challenged as you read these pages. May you feel the discomfort that leads to growth. May your life be forever changed.

With the Love of Christ,
Aileen Price

Spring Cleaning *Me*

1

A Time to Clean

This past weekend, the East Coast braced for Hurricane Sandy, a.k.a. "Frankenstorm". Rather than looking for something fun to do for the weekend, I spent the time preparing for the storm. It was predicted to make landfall after midnight Saturday night into Sunday morning. My husband and I purposely waited until late Saturday evening to pick up a few extra supplies at the grocery store. By eight o'clock in the evening, the crowds had dwindled down to a few scavengers like us picking through the leftovers. The store shelves were barren as people stocked up on batteries, water, paper goods, and non-perishable items.

While I had strategically postponed my grocery store odyssey, I focused on preparing the house. I wanted a clean house in the event we lost power. I wanted to make sure my carpet was vacuumed, the floors were mopped, the bathroom and kitchen were cleaned, and all the laundry was done prior to the storm's arrival. During my breaks, I'd read my Facebook friends' statuses, and I discovered I was not alone in the mission of achieving a clean house prior to Sandy's arrival. It was a frenzied attempt to brace for Sandy as if the superstorm were a house guest coming to inspect my home with white gloves.

The mission to clean was fueled by a nightmarish daydream in which I'd be without power for days. In this scenario, it would start out romantic and cozy. I'd snuggle under my favorite throw blanket with my husband and dog. We'd eat our non-perishables, cautiously rationing the supplies to ensure we'd have enough to ride out the storm. The sun would shine brightly through my windows bringing hope through its warmth. Suddenly, the sun's rays would illuminate all the dust that had accumulated on my furniture and kitchen appliances. I would obsess over the tiny paw prints on the laminate floor. Goodbye romantic candle light and snuggling! Enter the regret of having had fun on the weekend instead of cleaning the house. Since this scenario seemed highly plausible, I became determined to create a more pleasant possibility.

Have you ever been in a room where the sun's rays reveal dust you hadn't noticed the previous hundred times you'd been there? It's amazing what sunlight will reveal. Some people will react in shock and denial at what they discover. Others become horrified and ashamed they haven't noticed the dust. I know people who become visibly distraught and overwhelmed by maintaining a clean home. Other folks just clean up whatever's unveiled by the sun light. There are those who respond with apathy and postpone cleaning at their own convenience. Even others wait for someone else to clean.

The Bible says you and I are a dwelling. We're referred to as the Temple of the Holy Spirit (1 Corinthians 6:19). He lives within us. He has unpacked His bags, and the move is official. He's not a house guest. He will shine His holy light to keep darkness from our spirits just as the sunlight reveals dirt and grime. Like houses require regular maintenance and cleaning, so do our lives. To maintain a clean temple is quite different from a frenzied cleaning prior to a visitor, or Frankenstorm. There are advantages to keeping ourselves clean. We will do our purpose a favor by making sure we remove clutter and grime from our souls. It gives us the opportunity to maximize our effectiveness, providing us with the greatest opportunity to reach full potential in God.

We are all in various stages of our Christian walk. God is gracious to meet us exactly where we are. It's comforting to know that He doesn't compare our progress to anyone else's. When He created you and me, He had a particular purpose in mind. As we grow and mature, His plan for our lives will not change, even if we make poor choices along the way. He's able to forgive us and to guide us, to lead us and teach us if our hearts are humble (Proverbs 3:34; Psalm 23:3b; 1 John 1:9).

As we mature in our Christian walk, we need to behave like grownups (1 Corinthians 13:11). As we continue to walk with the Lord, we have an obligation to take ownership of our spiritual and personal maturation, and we have to embrace the development of maturity. Oftentimes, we can become complacent. God's grace is no excuse to harbor ungodly behavior and attitudes.

The easiest ones to harbor are the ones that lie deep within our hearts and minds—those that can't be seen. We can become skilled at putting on a facade, which may fool others. If we succumb to the temptation of comparing ourselves to others, we may find justification for our complacency. Scripture reveals God is equally concerned with our actions as well as what lies within us because any trace of ungodliness can derail purpose.

On one occasion, Jesus tells a parable about a Pharisee who was comparing himself to a tax collector (Luke 18:9-14) to confront "who were confident of their own righteousness and looked down on everybody else" (vv 9). In this particular passage, not only was the Pharisee comparing himself to "sinners," but he was also boasting to God about being better than they were. Although we are to watch our actions, Jesus taught us God is concerned about the attitudes of our hearts, the thoughts of our minds, and the utterings of our mouths. Though our actions may conform to what religion applauds as reaching the pinnacle of spiritual maturity, God looks upon the heart (1 Samuel 16:7). He's not impressed by our interpretation of righteousness; it's like filthy rags to Him (Isaiah 64:6).

Though no one is perfect, our goal as Christians should be to become like Jesus, especially if our goal is to embrace our purpose wholeheartedly. Self-manufactured righteousness will not bring us closer to this goal. Jesus modeled a fruitful, highly effective life. He never lost sight of His purpose. He desired the Father's will of to be done (Matthew 6:9-10; Luke 22:42). We are admonished to keep our eyes on Jesus (Hebrews 12:1-2), who kept His eyes on the Father.

If we become complacent Christians, we run the risk of becoming ineffective. A complacent Christian risks the opportunity to reach full potential in Christ. The greatest danger posed by complacency is the possibility of growing lukewarm (Revelations 3:15-16). Lukewarm is that stage when a Christian is no longer on fire for God. A lukewarm Christian knows all the right things to say and do, yet the individual is not in a right relationship with God. Some symptoms of this person may be one who talks to God in prayer but who does not listen to Him. Another example is a person who begins to focus more on personal happiness and goals, putting God's will secondary. Their use of time demonstrates a shift in priorities.

Those ready and willing to be vessels in God's hands must put Him first. Then, there comes a time of preparation. It will include time spent with God in one-on-one training. During preparation, the Lord will continue to refine His workers by gradually stripping away layers of worldliness in their lives (Hebrews 12:1; Romans 12:1-2). While spending time with the Lord, we will begin to understand His thoughts and His heart. As we begin to learn His will and to walk in it, we will easily learn that He desires for us to become more like Him and less like the godless pattern of the world.

When I began to spend more time with the Lord, I began to change. Things I once obsessed over no longer dominated my thoughts. I began to refocus my energy into the Lord's will for my life. For many years, I lusted over a high-powered career and an exciting life filled with travel to exotic places. Having a great career and enjoying travel aren't inherently wrong. I realized that service to the Lord and my place within the body of Christ (1 Corinthians 12:12-20) was not my priority. Upon becoming disillusioned with my fruitless attempts to craft my dream life, I began to spend time with God, not asking Him to give me all my wants but asking Him what He wanted. In His presence, I became focused on His will rather than mine.

He showed me that I had allowed the American Dream to become a god. Prayer and meditation on the Word led to a paradigm shift that filled me with new aspirations, and these aspirations filled me with joy, unlike anything I'd ever experienced. I had found my calling! Although Jesus came to give us an abundant life, pursuing my perception of an abundant life instead of His left me unbalanced and unhappy. In refocusing, I remembered the following: this life on earth is temporary. We have an eternal life. The Lord sent us here with a purpose. The Father has promised to take care of our needs and to give us the desires of our hearts when we seek Him.

Another outcome of spending time with the Lord was learning I wasted time pondering things that deserved none of my attention because they were unedifying and harmful. Thoughts of revenge, which I tried to justify as a desire for "justice", began to have less importance to me. The pain of the past suddenly became minor in comparison to the greatness of God and what He wanted for me and from me. I decided that I had more important things to do with my time than to rehash the past.

As I allowed the Lord to refocus my heart on His goals, and as I allowed Him to become my focus, I began to experience a liberty that I'd never experienced before. I found that He was able to use me in ways that incorporated my talents and passion. I went from feeling stagnant to making progress in life.

Q: What is your house cleaning regime?

Q: How do you react when you discover dirt?

Q: What would God's light reveal in you?

Q: On a scale of 1-10, how satisfied are you with your life? What would make your life better?

Q: How might your goals conflict with God's will for your life?

Additional Notes

Spring Cleaning *Me*

2

Are You a Spiritual Hoarder?

I've watched shows about hoarders. According to the programs, hoarding is now considered an illness. On these shows, there is an expert improving the hoarder's quality of life while diagnosing the cause behind the hoarding behavior. The expert typically advocates for ongoing therapy to work through the issues manifesting in hoarding.

What hoarders view as a valuable "collection" is typically an assortment of random things, including trash. Often, these homes pose health hazards due to trash, moldy food, and pests infesting the very places where they eat, breathe, and sleep. Mobility is limited. Stuff may be piled up to the ceiling. Some individuals have sacrificed their beds to their "collection". Others have lost relationships since relatives refuse to live under the same roof.

It doesn't take a degree in counseling to perceive something is wrong with the hoarder. Hoarders have trouble letting go of their "collections" even when confronted by their loved ones that they're living in unsanitary conditions or even after being fined. In some extreme cases, hoarders are on the verge of having their homes condemned. Looking through a spiritual lens, one can discern that the hoarders, in addition to individuals who exhibit other addictions, are trying to fill a void.

It's easy to view a hoarding program and feel far removed from the situation. We may even justify our own state of unkempt affairs by rationalizing that we're fine in comparison. However, I ask the following:

1. Are you hoarding trash within the Temple of the Holy Spirit?

2. Are you holding onto things that belong in the trash?

3. Is mold growing in your head or your heart?

4. Are you allowing "stuff" to pile up so high that you're risking your spiritual health?

5. Have you become so comfortable with the "stuff" within that it's become part of you?

6. Do you become defensive if someone you trust points out ungodliness in you?

If the answer to any of these questions is "yes," it's time to begin a thorough spring cleaning of yourself, the Temple of the Holy Spirit. The Holy Spirit is able to show you what lies inside of you that doesn't please God (John 16:13). Romans 8:27 says the spirit intercedes for us "in accordance with God's will". We have a powerful ally sent to us by God to aid us in the cleaning process.

He is an expert who uses no harsh chemicals. There are no toxic fumes or health hazards. Rather, He uses a gentle cleanser—God's Word, an effective cleanser that's as relevant today as the day it was spoken.

Living according to the Holy Spirit's guidance is an effective way to break away from living according to the flesh; living His way is the best way to ensure a hindrance-free life. He gives us a change of focus from the desires of human nature, which only lead to death, to the desires of the Spirit (Romans 8:5). If you feel bound by the "stuff" you're storing within you, I encourage you to study the book of Romans. In the eighth chapter of Romans, the apostle Paul focuses on the freedom achieved through living in the Spirit in contrast to the bondage of living according to the sin nature. With Jesus as our master, sin has no power to rule our lives. It's time to live in the full freedom for which Christ died. It's time to live a joyful, unfettered life.

In the coming chapters, we will explore things we may hoard within us, things that serve no other purpose than to keep us stuck when we could be experiencing amazing freedom in God. As we explore the concept of undergoing a spring cleaning, we will focus on the following three areas of the Temple of Holy Spirit: the head, the heart, and the mouth. For each area, there will be a discussion of the things we may be hoarding as well as a plan to achieve cleanliness in that area.

Q: What comes to mind when you think of being the Temple of the Holy Spirit?

Q: What do you hoard within you?

Q: What may be holding you back from experiencing full freedom in God?

Q: What would it take to achieve a joyful, unfettered, and purpose-filled life?

Q: How do you view the Holy Spirit's role in a spiritual spring cleaning?

Additional Notes

Spring Cleaning *Me*

3

It Takes Humility and Trust

Just as we periodically embark on a cleaning crusade to rid our homes of dust bunnies and spider webs, we should set aside time to clean ourselves. There is a man who was described in the Bible as a "man after [God's] his own heart" (I Samuel 13:14). That man was King David, a shepherd boy whom the Lord hand selected to rule over His people. What a daunting purpose for a boy! In Psalm 139:23-24, King David says, "Search me, O God, and know my heart; test me and know my anxious thoughts. See if there is any offensive way in me, and lead me in the way everlasting."

Even with God's seal of approval upon his life, David understood there existed a possibility he could be harboring something offensive to the Lord. He was humble enough to realize that he wasn't perfect and to ask the Lord to reveal anything that might be a hindrance in his life. He realized that only the Lord could help him rid his life of any offensive way. David has always been one of my Bible heroes. In recent study of his life, his humility has been remarkable. It set him apart. He waited patiently for his time to reign as king, even maintaining loyalty to King Saul whose reign was becoming a train wreck and who had God's Spirit stripped from him due to his own arrogant, rebellious choices. David's humility kept him teachable (1 Samuel 24:3-7; 1 Samuel 24:9-10; 2 Samuel 12:1-13). David became a successful warrior and a strong king. Unfortunately, in his later years, the ungodliness in his heart opened the door to disasters in his house and his kingdom.

In following King David's example, it takes a humble, willing heart to make Psalm 139:23-24 a personal prayer to the Lord. Clinging to pride will do no good; it will only prevent us from growing. Humility will bring us to a place of vulnerability, where the possibility exists that we may be confronted with hard truths. We may not be ready to face them; we may not even want to face them. Vulnerability can be frightening place for those who fear being taken advantage of or becoming hurt. In contrast, vulnerability before the Lord, our Creator, is safe. His Word says that He intends us no harm (Jeremiah 29:11). We don't have to protect ourselves from God. He has no ulterior motives. We have to trust that whatever He reveals is for our betterment and our growth.

Even though I knew God was concerned about me, I was afraid to approach Him. Deep down, I had an image of a God who wouldn't tolerate a person like me with human weaknesses. I feared that He would find things disqualifying me from His love. I thought He would scold me into shaping up "or else". As I've gotten to know Him more, I've learned the Lord is different from the frightening image I held of Him for many years. He's no intolerant, authoritative figure.

Through sermons, Bible reading, and prayer, I've learned the following: God is invested in our growth and our reaching full potential. Philippians 1:6 says "[…] being confident of this, that He who began a good work in you will carry it on to completion until the day of Christ Jesus." God does not begin a work in a person to change His mind, throw up His hands in frustration, and walk away. He is not sitting on His throne, with His index finger on a big red button waiting for us to mess up so He can banish us into eternal damnation.

People who earnestly seek to live a life pleasing to God receive no condemnation for human struggles. However, a person who continually sins with no regard to God's laws or one who offers insincere repentance from the lips but not from the heart will find judgment. Finally, I learned that God's trials are a training academy, not intended to disqualify us but to qualify us and to promote us toward His purpose for our lives.

As I learned about God's nature and His heart toward His children, I began to approach God with less fear, understanding He doesn't abuse His children. Rather, He wants to lovingly guide us over the pathways life (Psalm 25:4-7). If we maintain an erroneous impression of Him, we'll miss His loving work in us — the transformation of our lives.

Q: How can you make Psalm 139:23-24 a personal prayer to the Lord?

Q: What's the benefit of allowing Him to search you and know you?

Q: How would you define humility and trust?

Q: What "offensive ways" are you aware of in your life?

Q: What fears do you have about letting God search you and know you?

Additional Notes

Spring Cleaning *Me*

4

Act on It

"Knowledge is power". I heard an executive coach say, "Applied knowledge is power." The difference between these two statements is action – it's what you do with what you know. The account of the rich young ruler found in Luke 18:18-25 serves as an example to apply what we know. I honestly believe this man approached Jesus with sincerity in his heart. He truly desired to know what he needed to do to be saved. Jesus told him to follow the Ten Commandments.

What happens next is quite interesting. After the rich young ruler states that he had kept the Ten Commandments since his youth, Jesus identified that he still lacked something. Jesus asks him to sacrifice his possessions to meet the needs of the poor. Jesus told him what he needed to do, but the rich young ruler didn't care for Jesus' answer. The Lord's words were not palatable to him, and he left saddened. Ironically, *he* initiated the conversation with Jesus. A hunger within him compelled him to seek the Master. Otherwise, he would have remained content keeping the Ten Commandments without seeking further guidance. He was right to approach Jesus. However, following through with the Lord's commands would have given him a more meaningful and purpose-filled life.

If we are truly sincere in our desire to grow in our purpose and we approach the Lord with the humility of King David, we must be willing to act upon the instructions He gives. Once God shows you things in your life that are not pleasing to Him, what are you going to do? Will you feel sorry for yourself? Will you walk away saddened like the rich young ruler did? What keeps people from acting on what has been revealed by the Holy Spirit of God? Let's look at several possibilities. This is in no way meant to be an all-encompassing list.

Good ol' pride can get in the way. Maturity and growth have a caveat since we may begin to think we have nothing left to work on. We can deceive ourselves by thinking we've arrived at our peak holiness. Comparisons to other people become our crutch since we can always find someone who is in a different place in their Christian walk, someone who visibly exhibits a need for godly maturity. Consider the following Scriptures addressing the importance of having humility and making sure we don't have a false sense of achievement.

"If anyone thinks they are something when they are not, they deceive themselves." Galatians 6:3

"So, if you think you are standing firm, be careful that you don't fall!" 1Corinthians 10:12

"Pride goes before destruction, a haughty spirit before a fall." Proverbs 16:18

The proper attitude for us to maintain is that we continue to be imperfect people needing a holy God. The only perfect person was Jesus Christ. Our obligation is to keep our eyes on Him and to become more like Him, but we are not nor will we ever be perfect while we remain in this imperfect world.

Furthermore, we cannot afford to be rebellious and unyielding once God leads us to surrender offensive ways. The scriptures state that God disciplines us because He loves us (Proverbs 3:12; Hebrews 12:6; Revelations 3:19). For some of us, having God reveal an offensive way may seem demeaning. It's important to keep sight of His ultimate goal. We are His children, and He loves us. His motivation is to move us forward in Him, not to cause us harm. We're faced with a choice. Either we resist Him, or we obey Him by allowing Him to transform us into His image.

Secondly, some of us may become fearful of what we may discover. Sometimes, it's easier to remain the way we are because it has become routine and we know what to expect. We may become fearful of the work required to change. We may have developed some ungodly attitudes to protect ourselves. Responses to pain may be to put up walls, to push people away, or to withhold forgiveness. However, to live freely and have an unfettered, purpose-filled life requires humble dependence on God despite our inclinations and natural desires. In Isaiah 55:8-9, it says, '"For my thoughts are not your thoughts, neither are your ways my ways," declares the LORD. "As the heavens are higher than the earth, so are my ways higher than your ways and my thoughts than your thoughts."'

One thing that the Lord has impressed upon me over the last few months is how much He loves us. He does not minimize our circumstances, our pain, or our struggles. I have learned that I have resisted God or that I am tempted to give up because I have believed the enemy's lie that He doesn't understand human struggles. I say confidently that this lie comes from the enemy because the Word states otherwise. His Word says the following:

"There is no fear in love. But perfect love drives out fear, because fear has to do with punishment. The one who fears is not made perfect in love."
1John 4:18-19

"For we do not have a high priest who is unable to sympathize with our weaknesses, but we have one who has been tempted in every way, just as we are — yet was without sin."
Hebrews 4:15

Thirdly, a person may resist the Lord out of helplessness, a feeling of powerlessness. Revelation of an offensive way may leave a person feeling ill-equipped to deal with this new knowledge. During these times, remember there is nothing that we can accomplish without Him, in our own strength; however, with Him all things are possible (Matthew 19:26; Mark 10:27). The following verses encourage us to trust Him and to push fear aside because He is ever-present to guide us in the process of our cleaning. He empowers us.

"Jesus looked at them and said, [']With man this is impossible, but with God all things are possible[']." Matthew 19:26

"I can do everything through him who gives me strength." Philippians 4:13

"Have I not commanded you? Be strong and courageous. Do not be terrified; do not be discouraged, for the LORD your God will be with you wherever you go." Joshua 1:9

Finally, a person may resist God out of a stubborn heart. Some Christians are rebellious and prefer to live by their own rules. They take God's grace and freedom as license to stay the same. The saying is "Come as you are," not "Stay as you are." Any Christian living under this presumption should submit to God, the Master of us all. The throne of our hearts belongs to Him only. Paul tells us that we are not our own because Jesus bought us through His death, the ultimate payment for our sin (I Corinthians 6:19-20).

Q: How do you handle criticism?

Q: What can prevent you from approaching God?

Q: How do you identify with the rich young ruler?

Q: How do you view God's discipline and correction?

Q: What hindrances or obstacles keep you from acting upon God's instructions promptly?

Additional Notes

Spring Cleaning *Me*

5

What's on Your Mind?

"Finally, brothers, whatever is true, whatever is noble, whatever is right, whatever is pure, whatever is lovely, whatever is admirable – if anything is excellent or praiseworthy – think about such things." Philippians 4:8

If you're anything like me, you may find a discrepancy between what's on your mind and what Philippians 4:8 instructs us to think about. There can be a number of things cluttering a person's mind. We may experience reruns on the movie screens of our minds. These can be encouraging if we remember triumph or God's faithfulness. However, replaying unhealthy memories is time-consuming and harmful to our attitudes, in addition to being stressful upon our bodies. Most likely, you replay the latter of these.

We may have painful experiences that have hit a nerve deep within us. These experiences leave their mark upon our hearts. They are hurtful memories a person will likely replay. Because there is a time for everything (Ecclesiastes 3:1-8), I believe God allows us a time to feel the pain and to mourn (Ecclesiastes 3:4). There is a healthy time to make sense of the things that have wounded us. We need to learn from our experiences and our mistakes. Ultimately, there is also a time to heal (Ecclesiastes 3:3). Processing time varies for each person, yet there should come a point when the person moves forward from painful experiences. If we continue nursing our pain, we will block healing, which is God's desire. We can sabotage our healing by tearing open wounds mid-healing. Consider it may be time to throw away that old film and to begin playing a new one—God's plan for your life. God has given us medicine and scientific knowledge. If you need additional tools to heal, be proactive and seek out professional assistance.

REHEARSING

In Psychology, the term "rehearsing" is used to describe the act of replaying something over in one's mind. If we're rehearsing things that are impure, things that are not right, and things that are not lovely, we're in disobedience. Simply stated, we're in sin. The Lord gave us guidelines in His Word for our own good and well-being. Scriptures like Philippians 4:8 are not intended to censor our minds for the sake of exerting mind-control. Rather, He gives us guidelines because He knows the enemy can distort our thought life, enslaving us in past pain. Being past- or pain-focused robs us of the present, and it robs us of the big picture. Lacking Biblical perspective, a person might make poor choices derailing the reaching of his or her destiny.

Obeying Philippians 4:8 does not mean the Lord condones the wrong that's been done to us. He does not minimize our pain. Instead, the Lord desires to see His people walking in the freedom purchased by the blood of the Lamb. The shed blood was the ultimate act to shatter the curse caused by sin. The enemy wants to keep God's children enslaved. Since we are the Lord's, Satan has no legal right to enslave us; however, he can deceive us into remaining shackled by choice or through ignorance. In this way, he can distract us from God's purposes for our lives. Don't become a victim, a defeated Christian by rehearsing wrong thoughts. Know the truth so you may be set free (John 8:32).

We may never learn why God allows certain things to enter our lives. Even in the midst of difficult circumstances, we can hold on to the truth that God is good and just. While Jesus walked on this earth, He forewarned His followers that in this world, we would have tribulations (John 16:33). He was very honest about the difficulties of life and the challenges of following Him. He also offered words of comfort when He said, "But take heart! I have overcome the world"

(John 16:33). We can either get bogged down in the "why" of the situation, or we can trust God to get us through that situation. Though we may find ourselves wrestling with different issues, the principle remains the same. God is near. He cares. The Bible is truth, and if we seek His position on the issues of our lives, we can rehearse His truth.

THE TRAP OF WHAT COULD HAVE BEEN

Recently, I've been thinking about what could have been. I'm guilty of wondering things such as: "What if I hadn't done 'x'?" or "What if 'y' had happened instead?" We can get bogged down by a case of the "what ifs". There's nothing wrong with rethinking actions or behaviors to learn from our mistakes. Learning promotes growth. However, if we live in the *Land of What Ifs*, we're going to fall into a trap. We may become angry or resentful. We may fling ourselves off the rooftop of truth into the void of despair. Furthermore, dwelling too much on what ifs distracts us from the truth that God is ultimately in control of our lives (Psalm 139:16).

While it's true that we reap the rewards of our actions, it is also true that "in all things God works for the good of those who love him, who have been called according to his purpose" (Romans 8:28). Some of our circumstances are the direct result of choices we've made. Other things that have happened to us are outside of our control, like being laid off or becoming ill. Regardless of the reason behind our current reality, we have the ability to choose how we will respond to our situation. If your current circumstance is a direct result of a poor choice or sin, God is faithful to forgive you (I John 1:9) and to guide you back to the right path (Psalm 23:3).

Rather than focusing on what could have been, begin to focus on what will be. The Lord is not limited in His vision for your life (Jeremiah 29:11; Isaiah 55:8-9); with Him all things are possible (Mark 9:23). He wants to fill you with vision. Clearer vision will come as you clean out ungodly muck. When you surrender to Him wholeheartedly, you experience miracles. You will be amazed at His vision for you; you'll see yourself as He sees you. You will look back upon the painful, dark times, and you will realize that He carried you through to a better place. I often think of the poem "Footprints in the Sand". During our most difficult steps, He walks along side of us and carries us in His loving arms when necessary because He is our Father and He loves us.

In the next chapter, we will examine some biblical strategies to clean our minds. We are to put our faith into action (James 2:14-26); in other words, by cooperating with the Holy Spirit, we must proactively put an end to defeating thoughts. We have to be intentional in refusing to entertain thoughts contrary to the truth found in God's Word.

DON'T BELIEVE LIES

The Bible says that Satan is the father of lies (John 8:44); it also tells us that he is our enemy (1 Peter 5:8). There are many lies that permeate our culture. Unfortunately, as Christians, we're not immune to these lies. If we do not know God's perspective, revealed in His Word and through the Holy Spirit, we will fall prey to lies. However, we can inoculate our minds against the poison of Satan's lies. In 1 Peter 1:13[KJV], Christians are instructed to "gird up the loins of the mind". God wants us to protect our minds in the same way that soldiers protect the vulnerable, sensitive parts of their bodies during battle. The mind is vulnerable and requires the active protection of God's truth.

Let's expose some common lies that might clutter a person's mind and clean them according to God's Word. The following discussion is in no way intended to be an exhaustive list. Though the lie you wrestle with may not be listed below, apply the truth of God's Word to combat any lie the Holy Spirit reveals, and you will protect your mind.

One lie that we encounter is the issue of our self-worth. People struggle with the belief that they're worthless, second-rate. We know this to be untrue. In the beginning of the Bible, God called everything He created good. While it's true that humans are flawed by our sin nature, it is also true that we're viewed through the blood of Christ. We're told that we're co-heirs with Christ (Romans 8:17). God's children are called "saints, "chosen", and "elect". If you're a child of God, you fall within this category. Through His blood, you are worthy.

The following two Bible characters depict the struggle of how improper perception of self-worth caused them to voice objections to God's call upon their lives. The first is the prophet Jeremiah. When God called Jeremiah, he felt unworthy and unqualified to be a prophet because he was too young; yet the Lord reassured him that He handpicked Jeremiah even before he was in his mother's womb (Jeremiah 1:5). The second Bible character is Moses. When the Lord called Moses to lead the Israelites out of Egypt, Moses felt unqualified because of a speech impediment (Exodus 4:10). The Lord guided Moses to partner with a spokesman, his brother Aaron.

People have struggled with the issue of worthiness for thousands of years. It's nothing new. By studying the lives of Bible characters, we see the Lord's hand guiding them past their insecurities. Despite their imperfections, they fulfilled a vital role shaping Bible history. What is your role in shaping history?

A person may also struggle with feelings of unworthiness because of their past, their choices, and their sins. A low self-esteem is unbiblical because the Word reveals our identity in Him. Furthermore, humility and low self-esteem are not the same thing. Continuing to rehearse your sin in your mind is punishing yourself. It minimizes the power of the Blood. God does not condemn you. Rather than rehearsing a lie, rehearse God's Word.

"As far as the east is from the west, so far has He removed our transgressions from us."
Psalm 103:12

"There is therefore now no condemnation to them who are in Christ Jesus, who do not walk according to the flesh, but according to the Spirit." Romans 8:1[KJV]

"Then I heard a loud voice in heaven say: 'Now have come the salvation and the power and the kingdom of our God, and the authority of his Christ. For the accuser of our brothers, who accuses them before our God day and night, has been hurled down.'" Revelations 12:10

"[…] But if anybody does sin, we have one who speaks to the Father in our defense – Jesus Christ, the Righteous One. He is the atoning sacrifice for our sins, and not only for ours but also for the sins of the whole world."
1 John 2:1-2

Another lie propagated by the enemy is that total surrender to God's will results in an unhappy, unfulfilled life. In other words, this lie suggests we lose out on life by surrendering our will to His. Since the beginning of time, Satan has been drawing attention to what we cannot have or what God commands us not to do. In the tragedy of man's fall from grace, the account of the Garden of Eden, Satan asks Eve about the one tree of which Adam was commanded not to eat (Genesis 3:1). The Lord had given the first two people the freedom to eat of every tree, except for one (Genesis 2:16-17). *One.* Suddenly, that one tree became an object of desire.

In this account, Satan, the father of lies, audaciously implies God is a liar. When Satan tells Eve she would not die if she ate from the Tree of the Knowledge of Good and Evil (Genesis 3:4), no consideration is given to the long-term consequences of disobedience. Immediately upon eating from the fruit of the Tree of Knowledge of Good and Evil, Satan appeared to be correct. She did not drop dead on the spot. Unfortunately, this single act of disobedience has left its mark on humanity. Through this act were introduced sickness, death, pain, and suffering. Fortunately, Jesus revealed that He had come to give us life, and life abundantly (John 10:10[KJV]).

Today, some resist full submission to God's plan for their lives because they've become ensnared in this age-old lie and worry about what they might have to surrender. Recall the rich young ruler (Matthew 19:16-26). He appeared to want to follow Jesus wholeheartedly; however, he couldn't sacrifice his possessions. Although we make sacrifices when God asks us to surrender something, He rewards our obedience. Jesus calls those who hear and obey blessed (Luke 11:28). I'm convinced that God never asks us to surrender one thing without giving us something better in its place. His gifts are good and perfect (James 1:17).

Another lie people believe is that they're alone. There may be times we cannot discuss certain situations with people in our lives for one reason or another. Even during those times, we must stand firm knowing that God does not abandon His children. The Lord will never leave you (Deuteronomy 31:6; Hebrews 13:5). King David once said, "Though my father and mother forsake me, the LORD will receive me" (Psalm 27:10). He is a father to the fatherless (Psalm 68:5). You may have to undergo trials on your own for the purpose of your growth. You may find yourself alienated from friends and family at times. However, remember that you can always turn to the Lord. He will never turn His back on you. Best of all, He's always available. You are never alone!

A great man in the Bible felt completely alone — the prophet Elijah. Elijah stood up and defended God during a godless period in Hebrew history. At a time when a foreign queen introduced her gods, Elijah defied her false prophets, proclaiming the one true God (see 1 Kings 18:16-46). After this physically and spiritually taxing showdown with her prophets, Elijah found himself burnt out, feeling outnumbered by the godless people in the nation. He felt alone. All he wanted was to die. He fled to the wilderness, where God met him. The beauty of this encounter is that the Lord cared for him, sending food with an angel (I Kings 19:5-9), and He gave Elijah the courage to continue on his journey. He assured Elijah he wasn't alone assuring him there were seven thousand other godly people who remained faithful (1 Kings 19:18). Though Elijah felt alone in standing up for the one true God, he was not.

Don't believe lies about yourself or about your God. The best antidote for a lie is the truth. God's truth is a bright light that shines through the darkness; any lie that comes from the enemy is part of that darkness with which he attempts to thwart God's light. Just like the sinful nature cannot co-exist with walking in the Spirit, no amount of darkness can exist in the full light that comes from God (2 Corinthians 6:14; 1 John 1:5; 1 John 2:7-8). Allow God's truth to shine in you. Even when light reveals unpleasant dirt, have courage because He's there to clean you.

Q: What do you rehearse in your mind?

Q: How do your thoughts measure up to Philippians 4:8?

Q: How do your thoughts fall short of Philippians 4:8?

Q: What lies have you believed?

Q: Which Scriptures overcome those lies?

Additional Notes

6

Cleaning the Cobwebs of Your Mind

"Do not conform any longer to the pattern of this world, but be transformed by the renewing of your mind. Then you will be able to test and approve what God's will is—his good, pleasing and perfect will." Romans 12:2

Mastering Philippians 4:8 isn't something that happens overnight. Experts say that developing a new habit takes six weeks of daily practice. If you've been rehearsing wrong thoughts, chances are you've been doing it for a while, and you will have to be diligent about changing your thought life. The Holy Spirit is present and available, empowering believers to do God's will. No matter how you feel, you are capable of following God's will and having a healthy thought life.

It's irresponsible to expect God to clean the cobwebs of your mind if you're not willing to do your part. Here are some steps we can take to be proactive in our thought life. First, devote time to Bible study and prayer. Learning the truth of God's Word will give you good and right things to think about. You cannot possibly combat the enemy's lies if you do not know the truth. Meditate upon God's truth as revealed in His Word.

Spending time with the Lord will change you. When people spend time together, the influence they have on each other is noticeable. There's no better influence on a person than the Lord. Also, spending time with the Lord will change your priorities. Approaching prayer to spend time with God is very different from approaching Him with a wish list. It's biblical to bring Him our requests; however, our prayer time should include listening. We're never commanded to have one-sided conversations with God in which we're doing all the talking.

When we spend time with Him, we never know how He will aid our growth. He gives insight on our Bible study. We will understand things that were once confusing. He shows us how to apply the Word in our lives. He will often speak transforming truths that you would have never known. You may receive comfort. You may walk away with a renewed sense of purpose and clearer vision. You may learn of a hindrance worth hurling in the garbage. With Him, any day is trash day.

Romans 12:2 says, "Do not conform any longer to the pattern of this world, but be transformed by the renewing of your mind. Then you will be able to test and approve what God's will is—his good, pleasing and perfect will." Often people struggle to find God's will. Here's the recipe. If God's will seems elusive, perhaps you're conforming to the wrong thing. As I think about the meaning of "renewing of your mind" in Romans 12:2, I'm convinced that such renewal can only come from spending time with Him, in the Word and in prayer. If you realize you've neglected your time of personal devotions, don't beat yourself up simply remediate it immediately.

Secondly, memorize the Word. When you feed yourself on the Word, you receive proper spiritual nutrition. Scripture memorization provides you with quality information to store for later retrieval and use. David said, "I have hidden your word in my heart that I might not sin against you" (Psalm 119:11). Jesus effectively used the memorized Word. During His time of preparation and fasting in the desert where Satan tempted Him and distorted scripture, He was able to drive off Satan by rightly quoting scripture. Study Matthew 4:1-11, which gives the account of discourse between Jesus and the father of lies. If Jesus, God the Son, quoted scripture, how much more should we make scripture memorization a priority?

This theme of having the Word internalized was instilled in the Israelites early in their history. In Deuteronomy 11:18-21, the Lord says, "Fix these words of mine in your hearts and minds; tie them as symbols on your hands and bind them on your foreheads. Teach them to your children, talking about them when you sit at home and when you walk along the road, when you lie down and when you get up. Write them on the doorframes of your houses and on your gates, so that your days and the days of your children may be many in the land that the LORD swore to give your forefathers, as many as the days that the heavens are above the earth."

The Lord was very serious about making sure His people knew His commandments and His laws. We may say that He wanted his children to know Him and His truth. His Word is life (Deuteronomy 32:46-48). In addition, King David illustrates the importance of God's Word for the believer. He says, "Your word is a lamp to my feet and a light for my path" (Psalm 119:105). When your vision lacks clarity, His Word will light your path.

Thirdly, apply the Word. Second Corinthians 10:5 says, "We demolish arguments and every pretension that sets itself up against the knowledge of God, and we take captive every thought to make it obedient to Christ." As Christians, we have authority in Jesus' name. We have the responsibility to take action, even if those actions are internal and unseen, like decisions that need to be made. If we're careful to listen to the voice of the Holy Spirit, He will reveal when we're entertaining ungodly thoughts. When He speaks to us about these thoughts, we should respond immediately.

To take thoughts captive is to catch them so they're not running loose causing mayhem in our minds. The longer we allow ungodly thoughts to run loose, the more damage they cause and the further they lodge themselves in our minds. It's like postponing house cleaning. If you notice a drop of liquid on your floor and you wait to clean it, eventually, it's going to dry. Depending on what kind of liquid it is, the spot may even become sticky. When you finally clean it, you'll have to work harder than if you'd just wiped it right away.

Q: How quickly do you clean messes or spills at home?

Q: In what ways have you conformed to the "pattern of this world"?

Q: What thoughts should you take "captive"?

Q: What actions will you take when you recognize ungodly thoughts?

Q: How will you apply the truth of God's Word to your thought life?

Additional Notes

7

What's in Your Heart?

"For the word of God is living and active. Sharper than any double-edged sword, it penetrates even to dividing soul and spirit, joints and marrow; it judges the thoughts and attitudes of the heart." Hebrews 4:12

The heart is often associated as the seat of emotions. When we see a heart shape, we think of love. When we see a broken heart shape, we think of sadness and pain. The heart is also where our desires lie. Like our heart muscle pumps blood throughout our vascular system, our emotional center drives and motivates us. In Matthew 6:21, Jesus said, "For where your treasure is, there your heart will be also."

Like the thoughts of our minds, the contents of our hearts can be elusive. Jeremiah 17:9[NKJV] says, "The heart is deceitful above all things, and desperately wicked; who can know it?" The only one who knows the heart of man is God. Hebrews 4:12 says His Word judges the "thoughts and attitudes of the heart." Therefore, it's imperative that we open our hearts to the Lord so He can reveal any offensive way.

In Luke 6:44-45, Jesus explains that just as evil can come from our hearts so can good things. He says, "Each tree is recognized by its own fruit. People do not pick figs from thornbushes, or grapes from briers. The good man brings good things out of the good stored up in his heart, and the evil man brings evil things out of the evil stored up in his heart. For out of the overflow of his heart his mouth speaks." In summary, our words reflect what's in our hearts. We will discuss the mouth in more detail in chapters nine and ten.

THOUGHTS OF THE HEART

In Hebrews 4:13, we're introduced to a phrase: "thoughts and attitudes of the heart." Jesus mirrors this language in Matthew 9:4 saying, "Knowing their thoughts, Jesus said, 'Why do you entertain evil thoughts in your hearts?'" Matthew 9:4 creates a bridge between the thoughts of our mind and the thoughts of our hearts. We might say the "thoughts of the heart" are thoughts that we continue to entertain and become lodged in our hearts. If we don't "take captive" (2 Corinthians 10:5) offensive thoughts, we will begin to entertain these in our hearts.

The issue with the "thoughts of our hearts" is that if we do not guard our thoughts, we place a welcome mat out for the enemy, allowing him to infiltrate our innermost room. Jesus said, "For out of the heart come evil thoughts, murder, adultery, sexual immorality, theft, false testimony, slander" (Matthew 15:19). Let's compare Jesus' words to a documented list of sins that God hates (Proverbs 6:16-19).

There are six things the LORD hates,
seven that are detestable to him:
haughty eyes,
a lying tongue,
hands that shed innocent blood,
a heart that devises wicked schemes,
feet that are quick to rush into evil,
a false witness who pours out lies
and a man who stirs up dissension among
brothers.

Detestable things from Proverbs 6 overlap with Jesus' words in Matthew 15:19. Items in Proverbs 6, such as "haughty eyes", are mirrored in other passages as being offensive to the Lord. The Lord highlights pride as being particularly offensive to Him. He opposes the proud (Proverbs 3:34; James 4:6; 1 Peter 5:5). Jesus' list contains sexual immorality; warnings against sexual impurity are found throughout Scripture. The remainder of Proverbs 6 is a warning to abstain from sexual sin. People who profess to be God's children must guard their hearts against sin, especially those He has taken the time to highlight.

We may read these verses and feel removed from them. The first time I studied Proverbs 6, I believed all those sins existed in one rotten person. When I revisited this passage, I realized that though I may struggle with one of the seven, all of them disgust God. The Word shows us how these may appear in our lives, with deceiving subtlety. For example, Jesus said, "But I tell you that anyone who looks at a woman lustfully has already committed adultery with her in his heart" (Matthew 5:28). In 1 John 3:15, hatred is called murder: "Anyone who hates his brother is a murderer, and you know that no murderer has eternal life in him."

Though a person may not have physically committed a sin, we may sin through the thoughts of the heart. If we're not careful, these seemingly harmless thoughts can lead us to fall into sin. James 1:14-15 says, "[…] but each person is tempted when they are dragged away by their own evil desire and enticed. Then, after desire has conceived, it gives birth to sin; and sin, when it is full-grown, gives birth to death." Entertaining sinful thoughts and allowing them to infiltrate the heart is hazardous to believers. No one is above falling into sin. Keep watchful guard over your heart.

ENVY AND JEALOUSY ARE SELFISH

The book of James speaks much about the heart. A thread that weaves throughout the book is the role envy and jealousy play in a person's ungodly behavior. Here is another key to discerning the contents of the heart: it will shine through our behavior. The following passages illustrate this correlation.

James 3:13-16[ESV] says, "Who is wise and understanding among you? By his good conduct let him show his works in the meekness of wisdom. But if you have bitter jealousy and selfish ambition in your hearts, do not boast and be false to the truth. This is not the wisdom that comes down from above, but is earthly, unspiritual, demonic. For where jealousy and selfish ambition exist, there will be disorder and every vile practice."

This passage includes harsh words such as the following: earthly, unspiritual, demonic, disorder, and vile. Those words definitely indicate a need for cleaning—or purging. Another interesting correlation emerges is a link between jealousy and selfishness. A jealous or envious person is typically thinking: "What about me?" or "Why doesn't God do that for me?"

James 4:1-3 is a confrontational. "What causes fights and quarrels among you? Don't they come from your desires that battle within you? You want something but don't get it. You kill and covet, but you cannot have what you want. You quarrel and fight. You do not have, because you do not ask God. When you ask, you do not receive, because you ask with wrong motives, that you may spend what you get on your pleasures."

James 4 really speaks to a person's unhappiness when motives are wrong. First, God does not want us to be selfish. On the contrary, we're told to be selfless. The apostle Paul says, "Nobody should seek his own good but the good of others" (1 Corinthians 10:24). When we're selfish, our motives are wrong. When our motives are wrong, God is under no obligation to fulfill our every whim. When we're unhappy because we're not getting our way, we may resort to behaviors that wound others.

It's possible to become jealous of the person who appears to have the marriage that we desire. Perhaps we may become jealous of someone who's in a position of ministry we want. Envious, unhappy people spread their venom. Envious people become critical, judging the one who has what they want. They make comparisons to others. They may even sow discord. Perhaps they will behave inappropriately toward the person they envy.

I can share what envy did in my life. Establishing a career after college was a challenge for me. In contrast, my husband landed a great job before graduation. He grew within the company and liked his job. At first, I felt saddened that things just didn't seem to work out as nicely for me. Later, I began comparing myself to my husband in terms of number of degrees earned, languages spoken, and other skills. At this point, I became critical of him and prideful because I felt I had superior skills. As you can imagine, my attitude not only soured my behavior but it also hurt God. During this time, strife plagued my marriage.

When I finally approached the Lord in prayer, I realized that the reason my life hadn't unfolded according to my plans was because His plans for me were different. Though I knew He was calling me into ministry, I had been fighting full-time ministry because I wanted the stability of a traditional career to support my service in ministry. This wasn't what the Lord wanted for me.

One day during my devotional time, I became convicted about my career decisions. I felt God speak to my heart: "You're making Me your hobby." Ouch! He led me to resign from my full-time job. Though I knew I didn't belong there, it was a struggle to leave the security of a decent paycheck for the unknown. After my resignation, I began to train as a life coach and to take ministry courses. I'm pleased to share that I've become a certified life coach and a credentialed minister. I've had more joy and satisfaction in the last three years than I've ever had.

Prior to seeking and surrendering to His will, my heart was burdened by anguish, purposelessness, and bitterness. Life felt like a constant battle. Placing the Lord first in my life caused other areas of my life to fall into place. He has "turned my mourning into dancing" (Psalm 30:11). My life is far from perfect, but I can assure you that my worst day in His will surpasses my best day outside His will.

If you find yourself envying another person, quit being a hater and begin seeking His face. Rather than becoming bitter toward the person who has what you think you want, ask God what is holding back your prayers. You will find that when you approach God sincerely with an attitude of humility, He will speak to you about your situation, bringing clarity. Perhaps God can't give you the things you desire because you're proud and your motives are wrong. If you want glory for yourself, He won't bless you. You may find that what you want isn't right for you. Perhaps the ministry you covet would take more time than you can commit now and your relationships would suffer. Maybe that "perfect" spouse would be a complete mismatch for you.

Though your heart is in the right place, your motives are still wrong if you want God to do things your way. If you want to manipulate the situation to your own preferences, you will find resistance. You are not the boss of God. Be humble, and be yielding. For a situation to turn in your favor, you may have to change. To achieve a good marriage, you might have to change what's in your heart. To move forward in your purpose, you may have to yield your will to His. Be open to any change the Lord reveals as being essential to your growth.

FORGIVENESS

Forgiveness is relevant to me. I understand the struggle to forgive. I have read books and scoured Christian resources, in addition to studying the Bible. What I have learned is the following. Many people struggle with forgiveness. Forgiveness is messy, and it is a process. Forgiveness is a choice you make, not a feeling you experience. God commanded us to forgive *because* of how damaging it is not to forgive.

It's been hard to let go of the pain caused by slander and betrayal. My heart's desire is to please God in everything I do. I'd been harboring a strong desire to see "justice". I place the word justice in quotations because He's revealed that what I'd really been craving was revenge. I wanted to see my offenders suffer to the degree that I'd suffered. The Lord has revealed to me that, at times, I wanted "justice" more than I wanted to walk in obedience. Romans 12:19[NKJV] says, "Beloved, do not avenge yourselves, but *rather* give place to wrath; for it is written, 'Vengeance *is* Mine, I will repay,' says the Lord." Though we see a lot of injustice in this world, God's children have to believe that He is just, as revealed in His Word.

He doesn't do things in our way or on our time, but He is faithful. In everyday life, we understand that taking justice into our own hands results in negative consequences. If we become vigilantes taking justice into our hands, we will be prosecuted.

It doesn't pay to take justice into your hands. If we can understand this concept in the natural, we should realize that in God's kingdom, overstepping our boundaries has consequences. God is not pleased when we want to take justice into our own hands. God is neither incompetent nor a liar. If He says "I will repay," trust He will keep His Word.

The Parable of the Unforgiving Servant can be tough to swallow if you're struggling with forgiveness. Several years ago, I attended a seminar that included a lengthy discussion on forgiveness. The seminar facilitators made special emphasis on the Parable of the Unforgiving Servant (Matthew 18:22-35). Jesus taught about forgiveness by sharing a metaphor about the Kingdom of God. In summary, a king has compassion upon a servant who owed him a large debt; Bible scholars estimate this debt to be worth millions. He begs for mercy, stating he'll repay the king. The king is moved with compassion to forgive him and cancel his debt. The servant sees a fellow who owed him a few dollars in debt. Though the fellow begs for mercy, stating he'll repay his debt, the forgiven man casts him into prison.

Though the forgiven man owed more and had his debt cancelled, he had no mercy upon the other owing less. When the king finds out about this, he's livid. We read his reaction in Matthew 18:34. "In anger his master turned him over to the jailers to be tortured, until he should pay back all he owed." In verse 35, Jesus says, "This is how my heavenly Father will treat each of you unless you forgive your brother from your heart." This is a warning not to be ignored.

I've found the torture is real. One day, I had a revelation. I felt tormented and anguished for many years. As I thought about this parable, I identified the feeling of torment was related to withholding forgiveness. Simply put, unforgiveness is sin, and sin has consequences. Where there is sin, there is no peace because you build a wall in your relationship with the Lord. Where there's no peace, you will feel tormented. If your torment is a direct result of your disobedience, don't rebuke the devil! Repent of your disobedience.

In the Lord's Prayer Jesus says, "And forgive us our debts, as we also have forgiven our debtors" (Matthew 6:12). A few verses later He says, "For if you forgive other people when they sin against you, your heavenly Father will also forgive you. But if you do not forgive others their sins, your Father will not forgive your sins" (vv 14-15). Bear in mind that we're not perfect, and we can't possibly demand perfection from anyone. If you feel tormented, examine your heart to see if you're withholding forgiveness.

Because I'm experiencing healing through forgiveness, I would like to share a ray of hope with those walking the forgiveness road. The Lord is gracious. He will meet you every step of the way. The Lord knows your heart and your intentions. He isn't going to punish you because you feel pain. The key is to continually submit your feelings to the Lord. Submit them to His Word. For example, when you feel hatred, think of Jesus' command to love your enemies. It will feel unpleasant and unnatural, yet there is a benefit — you train your will to yield to His, which is superior.

As you continue to submit to the Lord, you'll notice He is faithful to heal *all* your wounds. Over the last several months, I've experienced the Lord's healing. I feel less pain. Though I haven't developed amnesia of the events causing my pain, the sting of those memories has lost its intensity. I learned that in my efforts to "protect" myself, I blocked my blessings, and I created barriers within healthy relationships. I've also learned lessons I was not ready for a year ago or even six months ago. The Lord will walk you through the process, without pushing more than you can bear. Be encouraged! It's possible to forgive and to find healing.

Another lesson I've learned is that forgiveness and reconciliation are two different things. There are relationships you will not be able to reconcile. I read a book advocating reconciliation as part of complete forgiveness. It urged readers to have a conversation with the other party and to restore the relationship. I closed the book never to pick it up again. The other party never wanted to speak to me, let alone restore a relationship. Therefore, according to the book, I would never achieve closure. I felt powerless; the situation was out of my control. The Lord taught me that I'm only responsible for myself. I'm responsible for forgiving the other party from their trespasses. By releasing them, it frees me. I'm not a failure because the other party is unwilling to sit down with me.

There are relationships that can't go back to the way they used to be if the other party is going to continue harmful behaviors. If you've been a victim of abuse, you need to establish healthy boundaries. You may have to keep your distance. Some people cannot be trusted. It's foolish to remain in an unhealthy relationship where you'll continue to be abused. God wants you to be healthy and whole.

The Bible gives us many guidelines on the types of relationships and people to avoid. The Proverbs and Paul's letters are some books which contain these guidelines for our protection. For this reason, you should not feel guilty if you need to end a relationship or you need to stay away from certain people. I encourage you to do a Bible study on the book of Proverbs so you can learn healthy boundaries in your relationships.

WORRY AND FEAR

Jesus confronts the problem of worry in Matthew 6:25-34; you will also find this account in Luke 12:22-34. His discourse is very applicable today. Jesus shared how God the Father knows what His children need and that He will provide for them. We are living in times of economic uncertainty. The conventional wisdom of secure investments such as real estate investments and the stock market proved to be dependent upon the overall economy. During the Great Recession, folks who were ready to retire had to stay in the workforce. I know a woman who owned multiple rental properties who faced foreclosure on her next egg.

Meanwhile, taxes are higher. Gasoline and food prices continue to rise. I hear many people voicing concerns over how they will pay their bills, medical expenses, and have extra money to save up for their future or for an emergency fund. We're definitely called to be good stewards of our resources. There are, however, situations that arise despite our proper stewardship. No matter what happens, we are still to cling onto our God who is our Provider.

Jesus addresses basic needs in Matthew 6:31-34. "So do not worry, saying, 'What shall we eat?' or 'What shall we drink?' or 'What shall we wear?' For the pagans run after all these things, and your heavenly Father knows that you need them. But seek first his kingdom and his righteousness, and all these things will be given to you as well. Therefore do not worry about tomorrow, for tomorrow will worry about itself. Each day has enough trouble of its own."

Today, He may be speaking to you about your transportation needs, providing for your children, or paying your bills. God knows these are basic needs, and He is able to provide for them. In return, He asks us to make Him first in our lives. When we're seeking first the things we need, our priorities are out of balance. When we're out of balance, we may miss the opportunity to experience the miracle of God's provision. We glean from Jesus' message that when we worry about tomorrow, we're wasting part of today. Finally, when we worry about tomorrow, we allow our hearts to be weighed down with anxiety, which also robs us of today. I don't know about you, but there's something unsettling to me about wasting time I can't get back.

Maintaining Appearances

Hiding or rationalizing offensive ways will only harm us. The contents of our hearts may spill out for others to see or they may remain well-hidden. Perhaps our words or actions will give us away. Though we may be able to keep them well guarded within us, we must remember that God knows our hearts. We are to guard our witness (Romans 12:1-2), yet we should be less concerned about other people's opinions of us and become more concerned about making sure that our hearts are right before Him. At the end of the day, you have to live with yourself in full view of your God. Worrying about appearances will hinder your progress. Decide to live unfettered and clean before your Maker.

Q: What do your words show about your heart?

Q: What do your actions show about the condition of your heart?

Q: What are your heart's desires?

Q: Who do you need to forgive?

Q: What needs do you worry about?

Additional Notes

Spring Cleaning *Me*

8

A Clean Heart

"Create in me a pure heart, O God, and renew a steadfast spirit within me." Psalm 51:10

To briefly summarize what we know of the heart, Jesus told us the kinds of evil that come out of the heart (Matthew 15:19) and that a good man can bring forth good things from his heart, while the evil man can bring evil from his heart (Luke 6:45). We are called to walk in the Spirit so we do not gratify the flesh (Galatians 5:16). We are capable of drawing from our godly nature or from our carnal nature (the flesh or the "old man"). Matthew 5:8 says, "Blessed are the pure in heart, for they will see God." A pure heart can only come from a person who is living to please God—that is, a person who is walking in the Spirit.

The Parable of the Sower exemplifies a truth about the condition of the heart. As Jesus describes the various types of soil (hearts) upon which the seed (the Word) may fall, we read the following. Luke 8:15 says, "But the seed on good soil stands for those with a noble and good heart, who hear the word, retain it, and by persevering produce a crop." The "good soil" is a person who has made an active effort to stand upon the Word. The other types of soil described — those along the path who have the seed stolen by the enemy; those on rocks who hear but have no root; and those among thorns who hear but do not mature — have the same ability to produce a crop as the good soil. Make no excuses for the condition of your heart. Decide to be a person who puts the Word of God into action in your life so your walk pleases Him, thereby producing a pure heart. If there is something wrong with the soil of your heart, allow the Lord to till your heart so it's prepped and healthy to produce good fruit.

There are things we can do to begin cleaning our hearts. James 4:7-10 speaks of humility and coming to God with a repentant spirit. It says, "Submit yourselves, then, to God. Resist the devil, and he will flee from you. Come near to God and he will come near to you. Wash your hands, you sinners, and purify your hearts, you double-minded. Grieve, mourn and wail. Change your laughter to mourning and your joy to gloom. Humble yourselves before the Lord, and he will lift you up."

This passage follows James's discussion on the motives of our hearts and reasons our prayers may not be answered discussed in Chapter 7. James 4:7-10 provides a practical outline on how to approach God when we're frustrated about not getting what we want. In order to make sure that your motives are pure and in line with God's, you need to approach Him in humility. Repent of your prideful management of your life, and seek His will for you.

"The sacrifices of God are a broken spirit; a broken and contrite heart, O God, you will not despise" (Psalm 51:17). The middle part of the passage in James describes genuine brokenness. What I mean by "brokenness" is coming to the end of yourself, your will, and your ideas in favor of Lord's; it's ceasing to resist Him. Our pride and selfishness hinder us more than we could ever imagine. They're like caked on grime, requiring "elbow grease" to buff away the layers. God's hand is freer to move in our lives when we're truly broken; otherwise, our resistance becomes a hindrance.

Another strategy that we can successfully employ to clear the clutter of our hearts is to stay focused on the big picture. Prior to Jesus' sacrifice on the cross, He began to speak to His disciples about being Kingdom-focused. He wanted them to keep sight of the end times. In Luke 21:34, Jesus says, "Be careful, or your hearts will be weighed down with dissipation, drunkenness and the anxieties of life, and that day will close on you unexpectedly like a trap." When focused on the big picture, it's easier to ignore distractions. The enemy will employ any tactic he can to distract you from your purpose. The Word is a powerful tool to keep you focused on God's will for your life.

Hebrews 12:1-2 says, "Therefore, since we are surrounded by such a great cloud of witnesses, let us throw off everything that hinders and the sin that so easily entangles, and let us run with perseverance the race marked out for us. Let us fix our eyes on Jesus, the author and perfecter of our faith, who for the joy set before him endured the cross, scorning its shame, and sat down at the right hand of the throne of God."

It's our responsibility to throw off hindrances and sin. We're on a mission, and we need to keep our eyes fixed firmly on Jesus. We have to make sure that we're clean and free to make progress. Don't allow your heart to become corroded. Allow the Holy Spirit to apply the Word, a gentle but powerful cleanser, to clean your heart so you can move forward.

Jesus used other opportunities to encourage His followers so their hearts wouldn't be troubled. He asked them to trust Him. He wanted His followers to live free of fear. His desire was for them to have peace.

> *"Do not let your hearts be troubled. Trust in God; trust also in me." John 14:1*
>
> *"Peace I leave with you; my peace I give you. I do not give to you as the world gives. Do not let your hearts be troubled and do not be afraid." John 14:27*

Jesus would not ask His followers to do anything they were incapable of doing. When He says, "Do not be afraid," He says it because He knows that through Him we are capable of casting aside fear. When He says, "Do not let your hearts be troubled," He implies that we have control over our emotions. We are able to let our hearts be troubled or not be troubled. Even when it's scary or hard, we can still have control over our emotions. How empowering!

Let's consider Philippians 4:6-7 which says, "Do not be anxious about anything, but in everything, by prayer and petition, with thanksgiving, present your requests to God. And the peace of God, which transcends all understanding, will guard your hearts and your minds in Christ Jesus."

Not only are we commanded to have dominion over our emotions, but we're also given the freedom to approach God with our requests about *anything*. We do not have to live burdened by our circumstances. We have a God who is willing and eager to walk with us. He promises to guard our hearts and minds if we come to Him with our concerns.

I had nightmares as a child. I remember waking up so afraid to leave my bed. I'd scream for my daddy. When I would call out to my dad, he would come. Sometimes mom and dad came into the room to see what was troubling me. I never remember my parents being upset with me because I called for them during the night. They never reproached me for disturbing their sleep. When my family came to Christ, my parents would pray with me when I had a nightmare. They would stay with me until I was calm and ready to sleep again.

I'm so grateful that my parents were understanding and kind when I called for them after having a nightmare. Our Heavenly Father is a perfect father. Just like parents love and comfort their children when they're afraid, He will comfort us and fill us with His calming peace when we approach Him.

The enemy wants God's children to live on the teeter totter of emotions. The more we're distracted, the better. He loves when our faith is shaken and our peace dwindles to nil. However, God wants us to be in perfect peace. Isaiah 26:3[NKJV] says, "You will keep him in perfect peace, Whose mind is stayed on You, Because he trusts in You." If you should entertain any thoughts in your heart, entertain those things that are true. Entertain God's Word. Keep your mind on Him and your heart filled with His Word.

Q: What distractions are vying for your attention?

Q: When have you cast your fears aside to move forward? What lessons can you draw from today?

Q: How can you know God's will for you?

Q: What's your definition of "perfect peace" as referenced in Isaiah 26:3?

Q: What hindrances do you need to "throw off"?

Additional Notes

9

What Comes out of Your Mouth?

"[…] For out of the overflow of the heart the mouth speaks."-
Jesus (Matthew 12:34b)

The Word explains how the thoughts of the mind can infiltrate the heart. In Matthew 12:34, Jesus explains that the contents of our hearts flow to our mouths, or our words. Jesus says, "But the things that come out of the mouth come from the heart […]" (Matthew 15:18).

The Bible has a lot to say about our mouths. We're given examples of what the speech of a righteous person should be—"a fountain of life" (Proverbs 10:11). We're even given examples of the types of speech that we should get rid of—"obscenity, foolish talk or coarse joking" (Ephesians 5:4). Furthermore, the Bible places emphasis on the power of the tongue. "The tongue has the power of life and death, and those who love it will eat its fruit" (Proverbs 18:21). We're also told that just like a small spark can start a forest fire so can the tongue corrupt the entire body (James 3:5-6).

I had the privilege of sitting under a pastor who devoted a lot of teaching to our speech. He encouraged us to speak life, not death. The more that I chewed on his teachings, the Lord showed me times when I was speaking death. To be more precise, sometimes my speech was negative, discouraging, and downright belittling. I can say that during those times, I thought I was in the clear because I was speaking truth; however, at times, my speech did not contain love. Truth stated in anger will only drive a wedge between people. Just because something is true, it doesn't mean you can be careless in your delivery. We're commanded to speak the truth in love (Ephesians 4:15). We cannot possibly expect to edify our loved ones if we're destroying them with words.

WORDS OF LIFE OR DEATH

Words of death often come during moments of anger or disappointment. These are uttered when we lose control. Words of death may include judgment and non-constructive criticism. They may be a verbal attack on a person or abusive speech. These are accusatory statements. Ultimately, these are words that crush a person's spirit.

It's important to make a distinction. Not all words that hurt a person's feelings are words of death. The truth hurts sometimes. Speaking the truth in love is not the same as sugar-coating. There is no amount of sugar-coating that can cover up some hard truths. Speaking the truth in love includes your motives in addition to the contents of what you say verbally or through your body language and facial expressions. For example, you may offend a proud person whom you must confront about inappropriate behavior.

A person may be hurt by your words even if you refrain from insults, accusations, and name-calling. Some people don't appreciate criticism, period. People who love you will be honest with you, yet that honesty may hurt. Proverbs 27:6 says, "Wounds from a friend can be trusted, but an enemy multiplies kisses". In other words, a friend may need to correct you. Though it hurts, a true friend wants what's best for you, whereas your enemy couldn't care less about your best interest.

Consider the following example. In high school, I had a teacher who told us that if we couldn't do well in her class, we would never make it through college. She went as far as to discourage students planning to become doctors based on their performance in class. Although I struggled with her class, I received an academic scholarship and made dean's list every single semester of the five years I was in school. A better way to approach the students would have been to encourage us to learn to study in a different way, the way that was required in college. It was inappropriate to tell us we wouldn't make it through college or to discourage students from becoming doctors. That was speaking death. In fact, I know a retired gentleman who was an average student in high school, yet he became a doctor, owning his own practice.

One tactic I've begun to employ is to pause and think, "Is there a better way to say this?" Often, I'll find that I shouldn't spew out the first thing that comes to mind. I took a theatre class in which we did improvisational exercises. We quickly learned that sometimes the first thing to pop in our heads was not class-appropriate. Our instructor gave us a piece of advice: never say the first thing that comes to your mind but the second. This advice has been a life lesson. If I stop to think about a better way to say things, I find that I can accomplish my objective without creating offense in relationships.

It's possible to speak life even when you're frustrated. We all know how to control ourselves under certain circumstances. There were times that I really wanted to unleash the fury of my words. I know that I have the ability to use my words as a weapon to crush any opponent. I've had this ability since I was in pre-K. However, when I didn't want to lose my job or have my employee record marred by a verbal outburst, I controlled myself.

It's easier to set my tongue "free" when I'm at home. After hearing many teachings about how we should be consistent in our speech, even at home where we let our hair down, I began to realize that I should treat every interaction as though the stakes are equally as high as potentially losing employment. Although we may become comfortable with our family and friends, we should offer them our best behavior, like we'd exhibit in other instances. Those relationships are precious and should be given the same, if not more, consideration than we would give an authority figure.

OVERFLOW OF NEGATIVITY

We are not called to be pessimists, speaking negativity. We're called to be people who speak the truth and whose hope is in the Lord. Don't allow your pain or disappointment to remain in your heart so long that your speech is filled with cynicism, sarcasm, or negativity. We're not called to be complainers (1 Corinthians 10:10; Philippians 2:14; 1 Peter 4:9). If we're really bothered by something, we should take our requests to the Lord or through the appropriate channels.

As a Biblical example, let's consider King David. He wrote passages in scripture that contain some of the darkest, most painful cries to the Lord regarding his battles in life and kingship. There's the key: David took his complaints to God. More importantly, he praised God knowing he served a powerful God capable of getting him through anything.

Hurt, disappointed, or jealous people begin attacking others through gossip, slander, or discouragement. Refrain from this behavior, especially in the church. If a person is set out on a journey ordained by God, be encouraging and supportive of your brother or sister. Don't become the devil's advocate in your self-justified attempt to bring "realism" to the situation. Even well-meaning people may discourage a person from their vision because something didn't work for them or another person. Previous failure doesn't guarantee another will fail.

Several years ago, I was leading children's church. I had a vision of what children's ministry could become. I dreamed of the day children would be part of skits and choir concerts. I shared this vision with a church leader who told me all the reasons why it wouldn't work. One of the reasons was that parents would not bring their children to rehearsal. A few months after that conversation, a couple partnered with me in children's ministry. They shared the same vision! Under new leadership, we saw this dream become a reality. The children's ministry is strong with their involvement in the arts; both the children and the congregation love their ministry. Being around people who don't share your vision is discouraging; however, the Lord is faithful to bring His vision to fruition.

There is room to bring correction; truth sometimes hurt. However, make sure that you, *Christian*, are being led by the Spirit rather than by your own imagination, experience, or opinions. If you are genuinely concerned that someone is making a mistake, present the situation before the Lord; ask Him to protect that person and to reveal His will. Encourage that person to seek confirmation from God.

The Bible is full of examples of people who were following directions from God that made little sense. Examples include a childless man who left his family traveling to a land he didn't know to become a father of many nations (Abraham), a man who built a massive ark large enough to fit people and animals during a deluge in a time when people knew no rain (Noah), and God the Son who became a man with no sin willing to die on a cross for a sinful people (Jesus). These are just a few examples of people who faced criticism and mockery for pursuing their purpose through faith.

Moses, the man whom the Lord used to deliver the Israelites from Egypt, faced much criticism from the people. In one particular instance, the Bible records that his own siblings, Aaron and Miriam, began to question his authority as the leader. Aaron and Miriam were with Moses throughout the entire exodus process. Miriam sang a joyful song celebrating deliverance from Egypt (Exodus 15:1-21). Aaron was Moses's spokesperson (Exodus 4:14).

Numbers 12:1-2 shares a conversation between these two in which they question Moses's marriage to a Cushite, a foreign woman. The conversation quickly turns to their questioning his authority based upon the fact that they too had prophesied. In verses six through eight, the Lord defends Moses. We're also told that the Lord's anger burned against them (vv 9). In verse ten, we read that Miriam was completely covered with leprosy.

The Lord is not pleased when His people complain against one another. It sows discord. In the list of the seven things God hates, it says He hates a person "who stirs dissension among brothers" (Proverbs 6:19). As God's children, we are "brothers" in Him. Just because we're living in a period of grace where we don't see complainers immediately stricken with leprosy, God's heart hasn't changed. What offended Him in the Old Testament still offends Him.

Speaking defeat doesn't reflect well upon our faith. Something needs to change if we're constantly complaining, weary, and defeated. Make sure that you're spending quality time with the Lord, like David did, bringing Him your issues. Everyone goes through trials of many kinds, but we're told to count it pure joy (James 1:2); we're not commanded to gripe to anyone who will listen. When you need prayer and support from your Christian brothers, get it. If you need counsel, get it. We're expected to carry each other's burdens (Galatians 6:2); that means we pray for one another during difficulty. However, make sure that you're also speaking the Word, speaking the promises of God, showing your faith even when you don't see a glimpse of reprieve from your problem.

UNEDIFYING TALK

Ephesians 4:29 says, "Do not let any unwholesome talk come out of your mouths, but only what is helpful for building others up according to their needs, that it may benefit those who listen." Some Christians' speech is no different than a non-believer's. Ephesians 5:4 couldn't be clearer about ridding our speech of obscenity and coarse joking. Such talk is so common it's almost acceptable.

I'm shocked at words tolerated on TV these days, words you wouldn't hear on prime time ten years ago. As it pertains to joking, just because something is funny, it doesn't make it ok. It's easy for us to tolerate inappropriate things if we're amused by them; somehow, we can justify it. Perhaps we feel immune, rationalizing that it won't affect us. Don't tolerate ungodly speech just because it tickles your funny bone. I'll admit I've had a good laugh over inappropriate jokes. However, there are plenty of other things to laugh about.

A person who spends time with God will learn what does and does not please Him. Never forget that

God is holy, and He has called us to be holy (1 Peter 1:16). To live under grace and freedom (Romans 6:15) doesn't give us license to tolerate ungodliness. It doesn't give us the freedom to use speech that is unwholesome, crass, or offensive. If these types of words pepper your speech, then I encourage you to spend time in prayer getting close to God's heart. Allow the Holy Spirit to clean your mouth out with spiritual soap. If you know that something is inappropriate and continue to say it, remember that we will have to give account for our careless words (Matthew 12:36).

Careless words also require change. These may include words you say without giving them much thought. These may be born in anger, out of frustration or when you're tired. Careless words can leave deep wounds in people; they can ruin relationships. Careless words are rarely edifying. If we internalize and commit to memory the fact that our words contain the power of life or death, we'll find greater strength to restrain ourselves.

To edify means to build up. The opposite of building up would be to tear down. God never wants us to tear anyone down. We have an enemy who does enough tearing down; we don't need to become his allies. Make it a priority to have your speech be a fountain of life that blesses others.

Q: Whose words have built you up in the past?

Q: In what way does a person speak life?

Q: In what way does a person speak death?

Q: What do you need to clean up in your speech?

Q: What unwholesome talk have you tolerated?

Additional Notes

Spring Cleaning *Me*

10

Clean Lips

"'Woe to me!' I cried. 'I am ruined! For I am a man of unclean lips, and I live among a people of unclean lips, and my eyes have seen the King, the LORD Almighty.' Then one of the seraphs flew to me with a live coal in his hand, which he had taken with tongs from the altar. With it he touched my mouth and said, 'See, this has touched your lips; your guilt is taken away and your sin atoned for.'"
Isaiah 6:5-7

Does your speech reflect your spiritual nature or your carnal nature? First Peter 3:10 says, "For, whoever would love life and see good days must keep his tongue from evil and his lips from deceitful speech." As Christians, we are called to guard our mouths. James 3:9-10 clearly warns against using our mouths to praise God and also to curse others. At times it would appear to be very easy to switch modes between praising God during a church service to speaking curses upon exiting through the church doors. However, James tells us that this is unacceptable. We can't afford not to control our mouths.

Isaiah 6:5-7 describes the reaction of a man who saw a vision of heaven. He realized how far he was from God's holiness, and he came under conviction due to his unclean lips. This is where Isaiah found and accepted his calling. Isaiah did not respond with apathy. He did not embark on a self-justification crusade. When Isaiah admitted his uncleanliness, the Lord ministered to him. Whatever purpose the Lord may be calling you toward today, whether it's stepping out into ministry or into a new phase of your life, know that He can purify you to make you successful in His will for your life.

The Holy Spirit will reveal when our mouths are out of line and our speech is not pleasing to God. Don't be surprised if He points out things that are not considered to be "bad" words or obscenities by our day's standards. He may convict you of the way you deliver your message. He may convict you of the harshness and judgment in your tone. He will open your ears to really hear yourself so you can detect words that are unpleasing to Him. Be open to changing whatever He shows you.

We are responsible for our actions and words. We have to learn how to guard our tongues. In Psalm 39:1, David says, "[...] 'I will watch my ways and keep my tongue from sin; I will put a muzzle on my mouth as long as the wicked are in my presence.'" David is very intentional about controlling his speech. There are days when we feel like our tolerance and patience are worn thin. In this case, we find another possibility. Psalm 141:3 says, "Set a guard over my mouth, O LORD; keep watch over the door of my lips." We can't expect God to do all the work. We must do our part and exert self-control; however, when we're weak, He is our source of strength.

To combat the issue of negativity in our speech, we should learn the Word of God and use it. For example, when you're feeling ill, you should proclaim what the Word says about healing; you can use a verse to declare the following: By his wounds, I'm healed (Isaiah 53:5).

A PRAISE MAKE-OVER

Transform your complaining into praise. It's counterintuitive to praise God in the midst of difficulty. When we think of praise, we usually think of giving thanks. Thanksgiving is part of praise. However, we praise God in the good times and bad times. We give Him praise for who He is, not just for what He's done.

As I began to study praise, I realized that praise changes *me*. It changes my circumstance through changing my perspective. When we're praising God with all our heart, we focus on Him, not on anything else. When we begin to focus on Him, we're reminded of His omnipotence. God is more powerful than anything you can go through. He is more powerful than a recession. He is more powerful than cancer. He is more powerful than your past. He is more powerful than the enemy.

The flesh does not want to praise God during trial, yet even in the midst of trial, we can learn from King David who said, "Why are you downcast, O my soul? Why so disturbed within me? Put your hope in God, for I will yet praise him, my Savior and my God" (Psalm 42:5-6). The flesh doesn't want to do many things, yet we manage to push past our feelings. If we can be disciplined enough to get out of bed when we don't want to but need to, we can apply the same discipline to praising the Lord when we'd rather complain about life. If we can push ourselves to go to work when we'd rather call in sick, we can praise Him when we don't feel like it.

DIG DEEPER

As we've explored the connection between the thoughts of our hearts and the overflow of the heart to our mouths, we should note that changing the way we speak is only part of our duty. We're told what does not belong in our speech. However, even if we manage to muzzle our mouths in front of others, we'll only accomplish part of the task by not changing our hearts and minds.

I encourage you to brainstorm with God when you hear yourself saying something inappropriate. Allow Him to reveal the source. For example, if you catch yourself nagging a lot, don't merely justify yourself and point a finger at the person or situation "making you" nag. Figure out why you're so annoyed. You may discover your nagging is a result of feeling unappreciated. That's something you can take to the Lord, and seek Him on how you can handle those situations. Allow Him to become the source of your validation. You might discover that you're nagging someone because you feel lonely and want more out of the people in your life. It might be an issue requiring God's healing and learning that He's always there for you. He's faithful to satisfy your needs and surround you with the right people.

I've had verbal outbursts that could have been avoided if I had just taken thoughts captive. During those times, the Holy Spirit has prompted me to change my thoughts. However, when I'm so intoxicated by my thoughts and don't take them captive, they begin to grow roots in my heart. My emotions flare up, and eventually, I have an outburst. In these instances, I realize that God provided me with the tools to avoid an outburst. I had all the resources to just stop thinking angry thoughts; therefore, the burden of responsibility fell on me. These are not good times. It would be much easier to obey and change my thoughts than to deal with the damage control afterwards. Though at the time I feel like I can't stop myself from thinking certain things, the truth is that the Lord isn't going to ask me to do something that I'm incapable of doing. With His help, I can do anything.

There have been times when I'm saying something that God wants me to stop talking about. I can feel this sense of needing to be cautious or to watch what I'm saying. If I don't stop, I'll deal with some consequence. There are times when I've felt sick to my stomach after saying too much. Other times my heart has felt heavy. There have even been times when I've bitten my tongue by "accident" after the Lord has urged me to stop talking.

There's no reason why these experiences need to continue. It's much easier just to obey the Lord and be silent when He prompts us to be. He's not the FCC. He doesn't censor us just 'cause. He gives us guidelines for our own good. What kind of example are we if we refuse to clean up our speech? How can we reach our optimal potential if we refuse to clean our lips?

Q: What can you do today to have clean lips?

Q: How would you describe your speech?

Q: How can praising God help you change your mouth?

Q: What's the benefit of digging beyond your words to identify the root causes?

Q: What resources do you currently possess to guard your mouth?

Additional Notes

Spring Cleaning *Me*

11

Kim's Story

Kim is a remarkable woman I met a few years ago. I would have never guessed her story. She had previously been diagnosed with leukemia. When she received her diagnosis, she felt compelled to find every scripture in the Word about healing. She made a list of those verses and confessed them daily. She believed God to be her healer. The result was that the Lord healed her, confirmed by blood tests.

Kim has graciously written up the story of her healing to bless you. Her testimony captures the essence of *Spring Cleaning Me.* It is just one example of how God can use the confession of our mouths to transform our current reality.

On April 16, 2008, I was six weeks pregnant, and I had my first appointment at the University of Michigan's

Hematology/Oncology department. I was pregnant with my fourth child and diagnosed with *chronic myelogenous leukemia*, a type of blood cancer. My physician told me that the best-case scenario for my survival would be to start treatment immediately so the disease would not progress since progression of the disease would lead to death. He also proceeded to tell me that I could not start treatment while I was pregnant. If I chose to continue my pregnancy, I would have to wait until my third trimester to start treatment. It would not only be risky for me and to the progression of the disease, but also the treatment would likely have medical implications for my baby. I had to make a choice to either take the advice of my physician or to stand on the Word of God and believe The Great Physician. He tells me in Isaiah 54:17 that no weapon formed against me will prosper.

I chose to stand on the Word of God, to meditate on it, and confess it daily. Proverbs 4:20-22[KJV] says, "My son, attend to my words; incline thine ear unto my sayings. Let them not depart from thine eyes; keep them in the midst of thine heart. For they are life to those that find them, and health to all their flesh."

On November 11, 2008, my daughter Rylie was born perfectly healthy without any medical issues. However, a few months later due to my postponing treatment, I had some complications. The first treatment I had nearly destroyed my liver. I became septic; sepsis is a blood infection that travels throughout the body quickly and can be fatal. I was hospitalized, given several blood transfusions, and taken into emergency surgery. I was then put on another treatment. Several months after being on the new treatment, the physician told me he thought I had mutations in my blood preventing this treatment from working and that he thought the disease was progressing.

For several months, I had more complications with my health. However, no matter how I felt or what I saw or heard in the physician's reports, I listened to God and stood on His unfailing Word. His Word says that by His stripes I am healed. Isaiah 53:3-5[KJV] says, "He is despised and rejected of men; a man of sorrows, and acquainted with grief: and we hid as it were our faces from him; he was despised, and we esteemed him not. Surely he hath borne our griefs, and carried our sorrows: yet we did esteem him stricken, smitten of God, and afflicted. But he was wounded for our transgressions, he was bruised for our iniquities: the chastisement of our peace was upon him; and with his stripes we are healed."

His Word says that Christ has redeemed me from *all* sickness and disease. Galatians 3:13 [KJV] says, "Christ hath redeemed us from the curse of the law, being made a curse for us: for it is written, Cursed is every one that hangeth on a tree." By His blood, He has bought me back, brought me back, and set me free from leukemia. His Word says that healing is part of the covenant, and I am under that covenant. Therefore, healing is my redemptive right; it belongs to me. It is mine and there is nothing and there is no one that can take that from me. Satan tried to steal the Word from me through fear and the things I felt and saw. The more I stood on God's Word, the more Satan came at me. However, God has given me power over Satan. Luke 10:19[KJV] says, "Behold, I give unto you power to tread on serpents and scorpions, and over all the power of the enemy: and nothing shall by any means hurt you."

I continued to confess out loud God's healing Word and to confess the truth over my body. I remember at one point saying, "God, I believe you," out loud hundreds of times a day—every time Satan would tell me the lie that I was going to die and leave my four children without a mother. Eventually, the hundreds of times a day turned to fifty, then twenty until I didn't hear Satan any longer.

During this time I had also received a *rhema* word from God. He said very simply, "My Word heals you." I stood on, meditated on, and confessed God's Word regarding His healing promises until it saturated my spirit. My healing was manifested from the inside out. I was healed spiritually first and physically second. God's Word *never* fails; it does what it says. Psalm 107:20[KJV] says, "He sent his word, and healed them, and delivered them from their destructions."

On April 16, 2010, two years to the day, I went to another medical appointment and sat in front of the same physician who told me the disease appeared to be progressing and things did not look promising. However, his words to me this time were the following: "I was very concerned for you, but you are now perfect, and you are going to live a long life without any complications. There is not a trace of leukemia in your blood."

I am thankful that I went through such a trial as this, and I am grateful that God trusted me with leukemia. Throughout this experience, I have learned that every trial we go through is an opportunity to give God the glory, and I consider it a privilege to be used for His glory. I would like to conclude with one of my favorite scriptures, Psalm 118:17[KJV]: "I shall not die, but live, and declare the works of the Lord."

Kim's story demonstrates how she chose to believe God. Despite her fears, she put her faith into action. Her mind, heart, and mouth were aligned with God's Word and the promise He had spoken to her. What would happen if *your* mind, heart, and mouth became aligned according to God's Word?

12

A Continual Process

"[…]just as Christ loved the church and gave himself up for her to make her holy, cleansing her by the washing with water through the word, and to present her to himself as a radiant church, without stain or wrinkle or any other blemish, but holy and blameless." Ephesians 5:25-27

Spring cleaning is an annual ritual for some people; however, it's not the only time of year when they clean their homes. Making sure that you, the Temple of the Holy Spirit, remain clean is a continual process. Today you can decide to undergo a deep cleaning of your soul to remove any contaminants from the world that hinder you from reaching your full potential in God. Set aside time with God dedicated to praying specifically about being clean before Him. Be willing to work patiently with the Lord as long as the cleaning requires. Allow Him to clean you as needed, as frequently as He determines.

Throughout everyday life, you will get dirty. Imagine the amount of filth our feet step on any given day. We have exposure to a lot in our external world, just as we do internally. Even if we were to confine ourselves to a bubble, we would still have to deal with the human nature in our hearts. Whenever we get unbalanced spiritually, we run the risk of walking according to the flesh and neglecting our spiritual nature. Because we're imperfect people, we need to continually allow the Lord to search our hearts and minds, revealing the things that need to be cleaned.

You will experience days when you will feel like you're moving backwards. There will be days when you find that you're changing to become more like Him; but on other days, you'll feel like you haven't made any progress at all. Don't be discouraged. In Joshua 1:9 God says, "Have I not commanded you? Be strong and courageous. Do not be terrified; do not be discouraged, for the LORD your God will be with you wherever you go." Joshua faced a daunting task to complete the exodus journey into the Promise Land. He had to pick up where Moses, Israel's leader of forty years, ended his journey. Becoming the person God intended you to be is a daunting journey. However, don't allow your fears to stunt your growth.

You will be tested to see if you're serious about your decision to be clean before God. When trials come against you, will you fall back? If you do fall back, will you stay down? The enemy will want you to think that you've wasted your time. He'll attempt to plant seeds of doubt in your mind about your progress. He'll want you to question the value of working so diligently. He'll want you to think that God is unreasonable in His demands of you. If you understand that you may face trials of this nature, you can be prepared to cast down those thoughts that only come from Satan.

This process isn't easy. You may be tempted to perform a surface cleaning by altering your external actions and to spray the air freshener of good works to bypass the process. At times, it will be so painful that you may even want to quit and stay the same. The advantage of persevering through the process is that you will come out a better version of yourself—a version equipped to carry out the purpose for which God created you. Any time you choose to become more like Him and like the person He created you to be, the more you'll flourish and prosper. Only when you're walking along the path of reaching your God-ordained destiny will you truly experience the satisfying life that you crave.

Spring Cleaning *Me*

The Pruning Plan

By Nancy Branton and Aileen Price

Spring cleaning involves cleaning the inside as well as the outside of your home. Outside we pull weeds, clean up flower beds, and prune trees and shrubs. The Word has much to say about the importance of bearing fruit (Matthew 7:16-20; John 15:1-8; Galatians 5:22-23). His desire for us is to yield healthy fruit.

To be fruitful requires pruning. Improper pruning will jeopardize your harvest. You risk yielding smaller, lower quality fruit. Pruning accomplishes focus on God's plan for your life. As you maintain focus on His will, you can begin to choose activities that bring you closer to His plan, thereby avoiding potential pitfalls and distractions along the way. To yield the best fruit requires simplicity in life and complete focus on Him.

The Lord's Plan	What kind of fruit does the Lord want you to bear?
	What is His plan for your life?
Pruning Distractions	What distractions jeopardize the quality your fruit?
	What needs to be pruned from your life to enable your fruit to be healthy, grow, and prosper?
Gaining Clarity and Simplicity *Imagine the pruned trimming falling to the ground, leaving behind a neatly dressed tree.*	How does simplicity impact your harvest?
	After pruning, what's left behind on your "tree"?
	What is the next step the Lord is asking you to take?
Motivation	What will you gain from embracing the pruning process?
	What will keep you committed to the pruning process?
Encouragement and Support	Who can support and encourage you during this cleaning/ pruning process?

When the Lord calls his children to walk by faith, oftentimes He shows one step at a time. By stepping out in faithful obedience, He will show another step. As the Lord reveals a new step, repeat this process to make sure that your choices and activities lead you closer your purpose. Be proactive to eliminate distractions and refrain from taking steps outside His will. By following Him, you will find simplicity and experience that His yoke is easy and His burden is light (Matthew 11:30). You will find yourself living an unfettered, purpose-filled life.

Suggested Reading

The following books were inspirational in my personal development. They served to prepare me as I developed both the "Spring Cleaning *Me*" conference, the inspiration for this project.

Adams, Stacy Hawkins. *Who Speaks to Your Heart? Tuning In to Hear God's Whispers.* Grand Rapids: Zondervan, 2010.

Andrews, Andy. *The Noticer: Sometimes all a person needs is a little perspective.* Nashville: Thomas Nelson, 2009.

--.*Time Traveler's Gift: Seven Decisions that Determine Personal Success.* Nashville: Thomas Nelson, 2002.

Bynum, Juanita. *Walking in Your Destiny.* Lake Mary, FL: Charisma House, 2006.

Cunningham, Loren *Is that Really You, God?: Hearing the Voice of God.* Grand Rapids: Zondervan, 1984.

Hagee, John. *Life's Challenges Your Opportunities.* Lake Mary, FL: Charisma House, 2009.

Ireland, David D. *Secrets of a Satisfying Life: Discover the Habits of Happy People.* Grand Rapids, MI: Baker Books, 2006.

Meyer, Joyce *Be Anxious for Nothing: The Art of Casting Your Cares and Resting in God.* New York: Faith Words, 2002.

--. *Beauty for Ashes: Receiving Emotional Healing.* Tulsa, OK: Harrison House, 1994.

--. *How to Hear From God: Learn to Know His Voice and Mark Right Decisions.* New York: Faith Words, 2008.

--. *Knowing God Intimately: Being As Close to Him as You Want to Be.* New York: Warner Faith, 2003.

Osteen, Joel. *It's Your Time: Activate Your Faith, Achieve Your Dreams, and Increase in God's Favor.* Brentwood, Tenn: Howard Books, 2010.

Ten Boom, Corey. *The Hiding Place.* New York: Bantam Books, 1974.

Spring Cleaning *Me*

About Coach Approach Ministries (CAM)

- Coaching that cultivates a person's or team's strategic and sustained growth and progress from a Christian worldview.
- Training for coaches who are thought partners with other Christian leaders.
- Credential preparation for coaches who are affiliated with the International Coaching Federation.
- Books for the development of Christian coaches.
- Christian Coaching Magazine, an on-line resource.
- Aileen Price's *Spring Cleaning Me* is CAM's latest resource for your growth and development.
- To learn more about CAM, visit ca-ministries.com/.